CIVILIZATIONS

OF AFRICA

THE
ASHANTI
OF WEST AFRICA

Jamie Hetfield

FRANKLIN WATTS
NEW YORK • LONDON • SYDNEY

This edition first published in the UK in 1997 by
Franklin Watts
96 Leonard Street
London
EC2A 4RH

© 1996 The Rosen Publishing Group, Inc., New York

Picture credits: Cover and pp. 4, 7, 8, 11, 16, 19, 20 © Jeffrey Jay Foxx;
pp. 12, 15 © Herbert M Cole.

A CIP catalogue record for this book is available from the British Library.

ISBN 0 7496 2862 6

Printed in the United States of America

Contents

Who are the Ashanti?   5

Where do the Ashanti live?   6

Towns and villages   9

Food   10

Kente cloth   13

Gold   14

Relations and families   17

The sweeping ceremony   18

The Golden Stool   21

The Ashanti today   22

Glossary   23

Index   24

Who are the Ashanti?

The **Ashanti** are one of many peoples who live in Africa. They are famous for making beautiful gold jewellery and weaving fine cloth.

The Ashanti are very proud of their history and **traditions**. Nearly 200 years ago, the Ashanti kingdom was one of the richest and most powerful kingdoms in Africa.

◀ The Ashanti have a long and proud history.

5

Where do the Ashanti live?

Most Ashanti live on the west coast
of Africa in a country called Ghana.
The capital city is Accra. Ghana was once
called the Gold Coast because there is
so much gold there.

Today, many Ashanti live in modern cities.
But there are some Ashanti towns and
villages in the country's rain forests.

Many Ashanti live in cities, ▶
such as Kumasi.

Towns and villages

Some Ashanti live in small villages in the rain forest. Footpaths through the forest lead from one village to another. Roads link towns and cities.

Village houses have walls of wood and clay. Leaves cover the roofs.

Inside, there are fireplaces painted with bright red clay. Pottery lamps light the houses at night.

◀ Rain forest villages are linked by footpaths.

Food

Ashanti men once hunted animals
in the rain forest. Now they buy meat
because there are fewer animals to hunt.
Ashanti women and children still catch
freshwater crabs and fish in the rivers.
Giant forest snails make a tasty stew.

The Ashanti are also farmers.
They grow crops, such as tomatoes,
cassava, **plantains**, oranges, peppers
and peanuts.

Maize is another of the crops that ▶
Ashanti farmers grow.

Kente cloth

The Ashanti are famous for weaving **kente** cloth. The bright colours and patterns have special meanings. For example, yellow means the yolk of an egg and blue is the sky.

Kente cloth was once woven from silk thread and worn only by the Ashanti royal family. Today, it is also made of cotton and can be worn by anyone.

◀ The Ashanti still weave their beautiful kente cloth by traditional methods.

Gold

In the days of the Ashanti kingdom, gold weighed on special scales was used as money. Little gold figures were used as weights. Some of these figures had special meanings. Today, many of these gold weights are in museums.

Now the Ashanti use paper money and coins, but they still make fine gold jewellery.

Ashanti goldsmiths are famous ▶
for their jewellery.

Relations and families

Ashanti families trace their ancestry through their mothers. In many villages everyone is related to the same female **ancestor**.

In Ashanti families the most important person is not the father, but the mother's brother. In fact, Ashanti boys often live with their uncles. When an Ashanti man dies, his wealth goes to his sister's sons, not his own sons.

◀ A family's female ancestors are very important in Ashanti society.

The sweeping ceremony

Being clean is important to the Ashanti because it helps prevent disease.

They have a special sweeping **ceremony** to clean a village of danger and disease. The women and children walk from one end of the village to the other. As they walk, they sing prayers and pretend to sweep the street with the brooms they carry.

Ashanti chiefs always wear something on their feet. ▶
If their feet touch the ground bad luck may come
to the village.

The Golden Stool

Most Ashanti have wooden stools decorated with beautiful carvings. The Ashanti believe a person's spirit has a link with his stool. No one sits on these stools.

The Golden Stool is the throne of a great Ashanti king who lived almost 200 years ago. It is covered in gold. When a ruler dies, the Golden Stool goes to the eldest son of his sister. He becomes the new ruler of the Ashanti.

◀ Because of their importance, stools are carved with great care.

The Ashanti today

Today, some Ashanti live in big modern cities and have jobs like everyone else. But others still farm and live in villages in the rain forest.

The Ashanti kingdom is now part of Ghana. The Ashanti are proud of their traditions and many think of their king as their real leader. They still believe in the power of the Golden Stool.

Glossary

ancestor   Relative who lived before you.

Ashanti   A people who live in West Africa.

cassava   Starchy vegetable used to make breads and other food.

ceremony   Formal acts performed on special occasions.

kente   Ashanti cloth with colours and patterns that have special meanings.

plantain   Starchy fruit rather like a banana.

tradition   Doing things in the way they have been done for many years.

Index

A
ancestors, 17
Ashanti kingdom,
    5, 14, 21, 22

C
cassava, 10, 23
children, 18
cities, 6, 9, 22
cloth, 5, 13, 23
crops, 10

F
families, 17
farming, 10, 22
fishing, 10
food, 10

G
Ghana, 6, 22
gold, 5, 6, 14, 21
Gold Coast, 6
Golden Stool, 21,
    22

H
houses, 9
hunting, 10

J
jewellery, 5, 14

K
kente cloth, 13, 23
king, 21, 22

P
plantains, 10, 23

S
sweeping
    ceremony, 18

T
towns, 6, 9

V
villages, 6, 9, 17,
    18, 22

W
weights, 14